MW01299724

Date:	Time:	Message:
Caller:		
Company:		
Phone:		
Email:		
Urgency: Low/Medium/High		Called ☐

Date:	Time:	Message:
Caller:		
Company:		
Phone:		
Email:		
Urgency: Low/Medium/High		Called ☐

Date:	Time:	Message:
Caller:		
Company:		
Phone:		
Email:		
Urgency: Low/Medium/High		Called ☐

Date:	Time:	Message:
Caller:		
Company:		
Phone:		
Email:		
Urgency: Low/Medium/High		Called ☐

Date: Time:	Message:
Caller:	
Company:	
Phone:	
Email:	
Urgency: Low/Medium/High	Called ☐
Date: Time:	Message:
Caller:	
Company:	
Phone:	
Email:	
Urgency: Low/Medium/High	Called ☐
Date: Time:	Message:
Caller:	
Company:	
Phone:	
Email:	
Urgency: Low/Medium/High	Called ☐
Date: Time:	Message:
Caller:	
Company:	
Phone:	
Email:	
Urgency: Low/Medium/High	Called ☐

Date: Time:	Message:
Caller:	
Company:	
Phone:	
Email:	
Urgency: Low/Medium/High	Called ☐
Date: Time:	Message:
Caller:	
Company:	
Phone:	
Email:	
Urgency: Low/Medium/High	Called ☐
Date: Time:	Message:
Caller:	
Company:	
Phone:	
Email:	
Urgency: Low/Medium/High	Called ☐
Date: Time:	Message:
Caller:	
Company:	
Phone:	
Email:	
Urgency: Low/Medium/High	Called ☐

Date: Time:	Message:
Caller:	
Company:	
Phone:	
Email:	
Urgency: Low/Medium/High	Called ☐
Date: Time:	Message:
Caller:	
Company:	
Phone:	
Email:	
Urgency: Low/Medium/High	Called ☐
Date: Time:	Message:
Caller:	
Company:	
Phone:	
Email:	
Urgency: Low/Medium/High	Called ☐
Date: Time:	Message:
Caller:	
Company:	
Phone:	
Email:	
Urgency: Low/Medium/High	Called ☐

Date: Time:	Message:
Caller:	
Company:	
Phone:	
Email:	
Urgency: Low/Medium/High	Called ☐
Date: Time:	Message:
Caller:	
Company:	
Phone:	
Email:	
Urgency: Low/Medium/High	Called ☐
Date: Time:	Message:
Caller:	
Company:	
Phone:	
Email:	
Urgency: Low/Medium/High	Called ☐
Date: Time:	Message:
Caller:	
Company:	
Phone:	
Email:	
Urgency: Low/Medium/High	Called ☐

Date: Time:	Message:
Caller:	
Company:	
Phone:	
Email:	
Urgency: Low/Medium/High	Called ☐
Date: Time:	Message:
Caller:	
Company:	
Phone:	
Email:	
Urgency: Low/Medium/High	Called ☐
Date: Time:	Message:
Caller:	
Company:	
Phone:	
Email:	
Urgency: Low/Medium/High	Called ☐
Date: Time:	Message:
Caller:	
Company:	
Phone:	
Email:	
Urgency: Low/Medium/High	Called ☐

Date: Time:	Message:
Caller:	
Company:	
Phone:	
Email:	
Urgency: Low/Medium/High	Called ☐
Date: Time:	Message:
Caller:	
Company:	
Phone:	
Email:	
Urgency: Low/Medium/High	Called ☐
Date: Time:	Message:
Caller:	
Company:	
Phone:	
Email:	
Urgency: Low/Medium/High	Called ☐
Date: Time:	Message:
Caller:	
Company:	
Phone:	
Email:	
Urgency: Low/Medium/High	Called ☐

Date: Time:	Message:
Caller:	
Company:	
Phone:	
Email:	
Urgency: Low/Medium/High	Called ☐
Date: Time:	Message:
Caller:	
Company:	
Phone:	
Email:	
Urgency: Low/Medium/High	Called ☐
Date: Time:	Message:
Caller:	
Company:	
Phone:	
Email:	
Urgency: Low/Medium/High	Called ☐
Date: Time:	Message:
Caller:	
Company:	
Phone:	
Email:	
Urgency: Low/Medium/High	Called ☐

Date: Time:	Message:
Caller:	
Company:	
Phone:	
Email:	
Urgency: Low/Medium/High	Called ☐
Date: Time:	Message:
Caller:	
Company:	
Phone:	
Email:	
Urgency: Low/Medium/High	Called ☐
Date: Time:	Message:
Caller:	
Company:	
Phone:	
Email:	
Urgency: Low/Medium/High	Called ☐
Date: Time:	Message:
Caller:	
Company:	
Phone:	
Email:	
Urgency: Low/Medium/High	Called ☐

Date: Time:	Message:
Caller:	
Company:	
Phone:	
Email:	
Urgency: Low/Medium/High	Called ☐
Date: Time:	Message:
Caller:	
Company:	
Phone:	
Email:	
Urgency: Low/Medium/High	Called ☐
Date: Time:	Message:
Caller:	
Company:	
Phone:	
Email:	
Urgency: Low/Medium/High	Called ☐
Date: Time:	Message:
Caller:	
Company:	
Phone:	
Email:	
Urgency: Low/Medium/High	Called ☐

Date: Time:	Message:
Caller:	
Company:	
Phone:	
Email:	
Urgency: Low/Medium/High	Called ☐
Date: Time:	Message:
Caller:	
Company:	
Phone:	
Email:	
Urgency: Low/Medium/High	Called ☐
Date: Time:	Message:
Caller:	
Company:	
Phone:	
Email:	
Urgency: Low/Medium/High	Called ☐
Date: Time:	Message:
Caller:	
Company:	
Phone:	
Email:	
Urgency: Low/Medium/High	Called ☐

Date: Time:	Message:
Caller:	
Company:	
Phone:	
Email:	
Urgency: Low/Medium/High	Called ☐
Date: Time:	Message:
Caller:	
Company:	
Phone:	
Email:	
Urgency: Low/Medium/High	Called ☐
Date: Time:	Message:
Caller:	
Company:	
Phone:	
Email:	
Urgency: Low/Medium/High	Called ☐
Date: Time:	Message:
Caller:	
Company:	
Phone:	
Email:	
Urgency: Low/Medium/High	Called ☐

Date: Time:	Message:
Caller:	
Company:	
Phone:	
Email:	
Urgency: Low/Medium/High	Called ☐
Date: Time:	Message:
Caller:	
Company:	
Phone:	
Email:	
Urgency: Low/Medium/High	Called ☐
Date: Time:	Message:
Caller:	
Company:	
Phone:	
Email:	
Urgency: Low/Medium/High	Called ☐
Date: Time:	Message:
Caller:	
Company:	
Phone:	
Email:	
Urgency: Low/Medium/High	Called ☐

Date: Time:	Message:
Caller:	
Company:	
Phone:	
Email:	
Urgency: Low/Medium/High	Called ☐
Date: Time:	Message:
Caller:	
Company:	
Phone:	
Email:	
Urgency: Low/Medium/High	Called ☐
Date: Time:	Message:
Caller:	
Company:	
Phone:	
Email:	
Urgency: Low/Medium/High	Called ☐
Date: Time:	Message:
Caller:	
Company:	
Phone:	
Email:	
Urgency: Low/Medium/High	Called ☐

Date: Time:	Message:
Caller:	
Company:	
Phone:	
Email:	
Urgency: Low/Medium/High	Called ☐
Date: Time:	Message:
Caller:	
Company:	
Phone:	
Email:	
Urgency: Low/Medium/High	Called ☐
Date: Time:	Message:
Caller:	
Company:	
Phone:	
Email:	
Urgency: Low/Medium/High	Called ☐
Date: Time:	Message:
Caller:	
Company:	
Phone:	
Email:	
Urgency: Low/Medium/High	Called ☐

Date: Time:	Message:
Caller:	
Company:	
Phone:	
Email:	
Urgency: Low/Medium/High	Called ☐
Date: Time:	Message:
Caller:	
Company:	
Phone:	
Email:	
Urgency: Low/Medium/High	Called ☐
Date: Time:	Message:
Caller:	
Company:	
Phone:	
Email:	
Urgency: Low/Medium/High	Called ☐
Date: Time:	Message:
Caller:	
Company:	
Phone:	
Email:	
Urgency: Low/Medium/High	Called ☐

Date:　　　　Time:	Message:
Caller:	
Company:	
Phone:	
Email:	
Urgency: Low/Medium/High	Called ☐
Date:　　　　Time:	Message:
Caller:	
Company:	
Phone:	
Email:	
Urgency: Low/Medium/High	Called ☐
Date:　　　　Time:	Message:
Caller:	
Company:	
Phone:	
Email:	
Urgency: Low/Medium/High	Called ☐
Date:　　　　Time:	Message:
Caller:	
Company:	
Phone:	
Email:	
Urgency: Low/Medium/High	Called ☐

Date: Time:	Message:
Caller:	
Company:	
Phone:	
Email:	
Urgency: Low/Medium/High	Called ☐

Date: Time:	Message:
Caller:	
Company:	
Phone:	
Email:	
Urgency: Low/Medium/High	Called ☐

Date: Time:	Message:
Caller:	
Company:	
Phone:	
Email:	
Urgency: Low/Medium/High	Called ☐

Date: Time:	Message:
Caller:	
Company:	
Phone:	
Email:	
Urgency: Low/Medium/High	Called ☐

Date:	Time:	Message:
Caller:		
Company:		
Phone:		
Email:		
Urgency: Low/Medium/High		Called ☐
Date:	Time:	Message:
Caller:		
Company:		
Phone:		
Email:		
Urgency: Low/Medium/High		Called ☐
Date:	Time:	Message:
Caller:		
Company:		
Phone:		
Email:		
Urgency: Low/Medium/High		Called ☐
Date:	Time:	Message:
Caller:		
Company:		
Phone:		
Email:		
Urgency: Low/Medium/High		Called ☐

Date: Time:	Message:
Caller:	
Company:	
Phone:	
Email:	
Urgency: Low/Medium/High	Called ☐
Date: Time:	Message:
Caller:	
Company:	
Phone:	
Email:	
Urgency: Low/Medium/High	Called ☐
Date: Time:	Message:
Caller:	
Company:	
Phone:	
Email:	
Urgency: Low/Medium/High	Called ☐
Date: Time:	Message:
Caller:	
Company:	
Phone:	
Email:	
Urgency: Low/Medium/High	Called ☐

Date:	Time:	Message:
Caller:		
Company:		
Phone:		
Email:		
Urgency: Low/Medium/High		Called ☐
Date:	Time:	Message:
Caller:		
Company:		
Phone:		
Email:		
Urgency: Low/Medium/High		Called ☐
Date:	Time:	Message:
Caller:		
Company:		
Phone:		
Email:		
Urgency: Low/Medium/High		Called ☐
Date:	Time:	Message:
Caller:		
Company:		
Phone:		
Email:		
Urgency: Low/Medium/High		Called ☐

Date: Time:	Message:
Caller:	
Company:	
Phone:	
Email:	
Urgency: Low/Medium/High	Called ☐
Date: Time:	Message:
Caller:	
Company:	
Phone:	
Email:	
Urgency: Low/Medium/High	Called ☐
Date: Time:	Message:
Caller:	
Company:	
Phone:	
Email:	
Urgency: Low/Medium/High	Called ☐
Date: Time:	Message:
Caller:	
Company:	
Phone:	
Email:	
Urgency: Low/Medium/High	Called ☐

Date: Time:	Message:
Caller:	
Company:	
Phone:	
Email:	
Urgency: Low/Medium/High	Called ☐
Date: Time:	Message:
Caller:	
Company:	
Phone:	
Email:	
Urgency: Low/Medium/High	Called ☐
Date: Time:	Message:
Caller:	
Company:	
Phone:	
Email:	
Urgency: Low/Medium/High	Called ☐
Date: Time:	Message:
Caller:	
Company:	
Phone:	
Email:	
Urgency: Low/Medium/High	Called ☐

Date: Time:	Message:
Caller:	
Company:	
Phone:	
Email:	
Urgency: Low/Medium/High	Called ☐

Date: Time:	Message:
Caller:	
Company:	
Phone:	
Email:	
Urgency: Low/Medium/High	Called ☐

Date: Time:	Message:
Caller:	
Company:	
Phone:	
Email:	
Urgency: Low/Medium/High	Called ☐

Date: Time:	Message:
Caller:	
Company:	
Phone:	
Email:	
Urgency: Low/Medium/High	Called ☐

Date: Time:	Message:
Caller:	
Company:	
Phone:	
Email:	
Urgency: Low/Medium/High	Called ☐
Date: Time:	Message:
Caller:	
Company:	
Phone:	
Email:	
Urgency: Low/Medium/High	Called ☐
Date: Time:	Message:
Caller:	
Company:	
Phone:	
Email:	
Urgency: Low/Medium/High	Called ☐
Date: Time:	Message:
Caller:	
Company:	
Phone:	
Email:	
Urgency: Low/Medium/High	Called ☐

Date: Time:	Message:
Caller:	
Company:	
Phone:	
Email:	
Urgency: Low/Medium/High	Called ☐
Date: Time:	Message:
Caller:	
Company:	
Phone:	
Email:	
Urgency: Low/Medium/High	Called ☐
Date: Time:	Message:
Caller:	
Company:	
Phone:	
Email:	
Urgency: Low/Medium/High	Called ☐
Date: Time:	Message:
Caller:	
Company:	
Phone:	
Email:	
Urgency: Low/Medium/High	Called ☐

Date: Time:	Message:
Caller:	
Company:	
Phone:	
Email:	
Urgency: Low/Medium/High	Called ☐
Date: Time:	Message:
Caller:	
Company:	
Phone:	
Email:	
Urgency: Low/Medium/High	Called ☐
Date: Time:	Message:
Caller:	
Company:	
Phone:	
Email:	
Urgency: Low/Medium/High	Called ☐
Date: Time:	Message:
Caller:	
Company:	
Phone:	
Email:	
Urgency: Low/Medium/High	Called ☐

Date: Time:	Message:
Caller:	
Company:	
Phone:	
Email:	
Urgency: Low/Medium/High	Called ☐
Date: Time:	Message:
Caller:	
Company:	
Phone:	
Email:	
Urgency: Low/Medium/High	Called ☐
Date: Time:	Message:
Caller:	
Company:	
Phone:	
Email:	
Urgency: Low/Medium/High	Called ☐
Date: Time:	Message:
Caller:	
Company:	
Phone:	
Email:	
Urgency: Low/Medium/High	Called ☐

Date:	Time:	Message:
Caller:		
Company:		
Phone:		
Email:		
Urgency: Low/Medium/High		Called ☐
Date:	Time:	Message:
Caller:		
Company:		
Phone:		
Email:		
Urgency: Low/Medium/High		Called ☐
Date:	Time:	Message:
Caller:		
Company:		
Phone:		
Email:		
Urgency: Low/Medium/High		Called ☐
Date:	Time:	Message:
Caller:		
Company:		
Phone:		
Email:		
Urgency: Low/Medium/High		Called ☐

Date: Time:	Message:
Caller:	
Company:	
Phone:	
Email:	
Urgency: Low/Medium/High	Called ☐
Date: Time:	Message:
Caller:	
Company:	
Phone:	
Email:	
Urgency: Low/Medium/High	Called ☐
Date: Time:	Message:
Caller:	
Company:	
Phone:	
Email:	
Urgency: Low/Medium/High	Called ☐
Date: Time:	Message:
Caller:	
Company:	
Phone:	
Email:	
Urgency: Low/Medium/High	Called ☐

Date: Time:	Message:
Caller:	
Company:	
Phone:	
Email:	
Urgency: Low/Medium/High	Called ☐
Date: Time:	Message:
Caller:	
Company:	
Phone:	
Email:	
Urgency: Low/Medium/High	Called ☐
Date: Time:	Message:
Caller:	
Company:	
Phone:	
Email:	
Urgency: Low/Medium/High	Called ☐
Date: Time:	Message:
Caller:	
Company:	
Phone:	
Email:	
Urgency: Low/Medium/High	Called ☐

Date: Time:	Message:
Caller:	
Company:	
Phone:	
Email:	
Urgency: Low/Medium/High	Called ☐
Date: Time:	Message:
Caller:	
Company:	
Phone:	
Email:	
Urgency: Low/Medium/High	Called ☐
Date: Time:	Message:
Caller:	
Company:	
Phone:	
Email:	
Urgency: Low/Medium/High	Called ☐
Date: Time:	Message:
Caller:	
Company:	
Phone:	
Email:	
Urgency: Low/Medium/High	Called ☐

Date: Time:	Message:
Caller:	
Company:	
Phone:	
Email:	
Urgency: Low/Medium/High	Called ☐
Date: Time:	Message:
Caller:	
Company:	
Phone:	
Email:	
Urgency: Low/Medium/High	Called ☐
Date: Time:	Message:
Caller:	
Company:	
Phone:	
Email:	
Urgency: Low/Medium/High	Called ☐
Date: Time:	Message:
Caller:	
Company:	
Phone:	
Email:	
Urgency: Low/Medium/High	Called ☐

Date: Time:	Message:
Caller:	
Company:	
Phone:	
Email:	
Urgency: Low/Medium/High	Called ☐
Date: Time:	Message:
Caller:	
Company:	
Phone:	
Email:	
Urgency: Low/Medium/High	Called ☐
Date: Time:	Message:
Caller:	
Company:	
Phone:	
Email:	
Urgency: Low/Medium/High	Called ☐
Date: Time:	Message:
Caller:	
Company:	
Phone:	
Email:	
Urgency: Low/Medium/High	Called ☐

Date: Time:	Message:
Caller:	
Company:	
Phone:	
Email:	
Urgency: Low/Medium/High	Called ☐
Date: Time:	Message:
Caller:	
Company:	
Phone:	
Email:	
Urgency: Low/Medium/High	Called ☐
Date: Time:	Message:
Caller:	
Company:	
Phone:	
Email:	
Urgency: Low/Medium/High	Called ☐
Date: Time:	Message:
Caller:	
Company:	
Phone:	
Email:	
Urgency: Low/Medium/High	Called ☐

Date: Time:	Message:
Caller:	
Company:	
Phone:	
Email:	
Urgency: Low/Medium/High	Called ☐
Date: Time:	Message:
Caller:	
Company:	
Phone:	
Email:	
Urgency: Low/Medium/High	Called ☐
Date: Time:	Message:
Caller:	
Company:	
Phone:	
Email:	
Urgency: Low/Medium/High	Called ☐
Date: Time:	Message:
Caller:	
Company:	
Phone:	
Email:	
Urgency: Low/Medium/High	Called ☐

Date: Time:	Message:
Caller:	
Company:	
Phone:	
Email:	
Urgency: Low/Medium/High	Called ☐
Date: Time:	Message:
Caller:	
Company:	
Phone:	
Email:	
Urgency: Low/Medium/High	Called ☐
Date: Time:	Message:
Caller:	
Company:	
Phone:	
Email:	
Urgency: Low/Medium/High	Called ☐
Date: Time:	Message:
Caller:	
Company:	
Phone:	
Email:	
Urgency: Low/Medium/High	Called ☐

Date: Time:	Message:
Caller:	
Company:	
Phone:	
Email:	
Urgency: Low/Medium/High	Called ☐
Date: Time:	Message:
Caller:	
Company:	
Phone:	
Email:	
Urgency: Low/Medium/High	Called ☐
Date: Time:	Message:
Caller:	
Company:	
Phone:	
Email:	
Urgency: Low/Medium/High	Called ☐
Date: Time:	Message:
Caller:	
Company:	
Phone:	
Email:	
Urgency: Low/Medium/High	Called ☐

Date: Time:	Message:
Caller:	
Company:	
Phone:	
Email:	
Urgency: Low/Medium/High	Called ☐
Date: Time:	Message:
Caller:	
Company:	
Phone:	
Email:	
Urgency: Low/Medium/High	Called ☐
Date: Time:	Message:
Caller:	
Company:	
Phone:	
Email:	
Urgency: Low/Medium/High	Called ☐
Date: Time:	Message:
Caller:	
Company:	
Phone:	
Email:	
Urgency: Low/Medium/High	Called ☐

Date: Time:	Message:
Caller:	
Company:	
Phone:	
Email:	
Urgency: Low/Medium/High	Called ☐
Date: Time:	Message:
Caller:	
Company:	
Phone:	
Email:	
Urgency: Low/Medium/High	Called ☐
Date: Time:	Message:
Caller:	
Company:	
Phone:	
Email:	
Urgency: Low/Medium/High	Called ☐
Date: Time:	Message:
Caller:	
Company:	
Phone:	
Email:	
Urgency: Low/Medium/High	Called ☐

Date: Time:	Message:
Caller:	
Company:	
Phone:	
Email:	
Urgency: Low/Medium/High	Called ☐
Date: Time:	Message:
Caller:	
Company:	
Phone:	
Email:	
Urgency: Low/Medium/High	Called ☐
Date: Time:	Message:
Caller:	
Company:	
Phone:	
Email:	
Urgency: Low/Medium/High	Called ☐
Date: Time:	Message:
Caller:	
Company:	
Phone:	
Email:	
Urgency: Low/Medium/High	Called ☐

Date:	Time:	Message:
Caller:		
Company:		
Phone:		
Email:		
Urgency: Low/Medium/High		Called ☐
Date:	Time:	Message:
Caller:		
Company:		
Phone:		
Email:		
Urgency: Low/Medium/High		Called ☐
Date:	Time:	Message:
Caller:		
Company:		
Phone:		
Email:		
Urgency: Low/Medium/High		Called ☐
Date:	Time:	Message:
Caller:		
Company:		
Phone:		
Email:		
Urgency: Low/Medium/High		Called ☐

Date: Time:	Message:
Caller:	
Company:	
Phone:	
Email:	
Urgency: Low/Medium/High	Called ☐
Date: Time:	Message:
Caller:	
Company:	
Phone:	
Email:	
Urgency: Low/Medium/High	Called ☐
Date: Time:	Message:
Caller:	
Company:	
Phone:	
Email:	
Urgency: Low/Medium/High	Called ☐
Date: Time:	Message:
Caller:	
Company:	
Phone:	
Email:	
Urgency: Low/Medium/High	Called ☐

Date: Time:	Message:
Caller:	
Company:	
Phone:	
Email:	
Urgency: Low/Medium/High	Called ☐
Date: Time:	Message:
Caller:	
Company:	
Phone:	
Email:	
Urgency: Low/Medium/High	Called ☐
Date: Time:	Message:
Caller:	
Company:	
Phone:	
Email:	
Urgency: Low/Medium/High	Called ☐
Date: Time:	Message:
Caller:	
Company:	
Phone:	
Email:	
Urgency: Low/Medium/High	Called ☐

Date: Time:	Message:
Caller:	
Company:	
Phone:	
Email:	
Urgency: Low/Medium/High	Called ☐
Date: Time:	Message:
Caller:	
Company:	
Phone:	
Email:	
Urgency: Low/Medium/High	Called ☐
Date: Time:	Message:
Caller:	
Company:	
Phone:	
Email:	
Urgency: Low/Medium/High	Called ☐
Date: Time:	Message:
Caller:	
Company:	
Phone:	
Email:	
Urgency: Low/Medium/High	Called ☐

Date: Time:	Message:
Caller:	
Company:	
Phone:	
Email:	
Urgency: Low/Medium/High	Called ☐
Date: Time:	Message:
Caller:	
Company:	
Phone:	
Email:	
Urgency: Low/Medium/High	Called ☐
Date: Time:	Message:
Caller:	
Company:	
Phone:	
Email:	
Urgency: Low/Medium/High	Called ☐
Date: Time:	Message:
Caller:	
Company:	
Phone:	
Email:	
Urgency: Low/Medium/High	Called ☐

Date: Time:	Message:
Caller:	
Company:	
Phone:	
Email:	
Urgency: Low/Medium/High	Called ☐
Date: Time:	Message:
Caller:	
Company:	
Phone:	
Email:	
Urgency: Low/Medium/High	Called ☐
Date: Time:	Message:
Caller:	
Company:	
Phone:	
Email:	
Urgency: Low/Medium/High	Called ☐
Date: Time:	Message:
Caller:	
Company:	
Phone:	
Email:	
Urgency: Low/Medium/High	Called ☐

Date: Time:	Message:
Caller:	
Company:	
Phone:	
Email:	
Urgency: Low/Medium/High	Called ☐
Date: Time:	Message:
Caller:	
Company:	
Phone:	
Email:	
Urgency: Low/Medium/High	Called ☐
Date: Time:	Message:
Caller:	
Company:	
Phone:	
Email:	
Urgency: Low/Medium/High	Called ☐
Date: Time:	Message:
Caller:	
Company:	
Phone:	
Email:	
Urgency: Low/Medium/High	Called ☐

Date: Time:	Message:
Caller:	
Company:	
Phone:	
Email:	
Urgency: Low/Medium/High	Called ☐
Date: Time:	Message:
Caller:	
Company:	
Phone:	
Email:	
Urgency: Low/Medium/High	Called ☐
Date: Time:	Message:
Caller:	
Company:	
Phone:	
Email:	
Urgency: Low/Medium/High	Called ☐
Date: Time:	Message:
Caller:	
Company:	
Phone:	
Email:	
Urgency: Low/Medium/High	Called ☐

Date:	Time:	Message:
Caller:		
Company:		
Phone:		
Email:		
Urgency: Low/Medium/High		Called ☐
Date:	Time:	Message:
Caller:		
Company:		
Phone:		
Email:		
Urgency: Low/Medium/High		Called ☐
Date:	Time:	Message:
Caller:		
Company:		
Phone:		
Email:		
Urgency: Low/Medium/High		Called ☐
Date:	Time:	Message:
Caller:		
Company:		
Phone:		
Email:		
Urgency: Low/Medium/High		Called ☐

Date: Time:	Message:
Caller:	
Company:	
Phone:	
Email:	
Urgency: Low/Medium/High	Called ☐
Date: Time:	Message:
Caller:	
Company:	
Phone:	
Email:	
Urgency: Low/Medium/High	Called ☐
Date: Time:	Message:
Caller:	
Company:	
Phone:	
Email:	
Urgency: Low/Medium/High	Called ☐
Date: Time:	Message:
Caller:	
Company:	
Phone:	
Email:	
Urgency: Low/Medium/High	Called ☐

Date:　　　Time:	Message:
Caller:	
Company:	
Phone:	
Email:	
Urgency: Low/Medium/High	Called ☐
Date:　　　Time:	Message:
Caller:	
Company:	
Phone:	
Email:	
Urgency: Low/Medium/High	Called ☐
Date:　　　Time:	Message:
Caller:	
Company:	
Phone:	
Email:	
Urgency: Low/Medium/High	Called ☐
Date:　　　Time:	Message:
Caller:	
Company:	
Phone:	
Email:	
Urgency: Low/Medium/High	Called ☐

Date: Time:	Message:
Caller:	
Company:	
Phone:	
Email:	
Urgency: Low/Medium/High	Called ☐
Date: Time:	Message:
Caller:	
Company:	
Phone:	
Email:	
Urgency: Low/Medium/High	Called ☐
Date: Time:	Message:
Caller:	
Company:	
Phone:	
Email:	
Urgency: Low/Medium/High	Called ☐
Date: Time:	Message:
Caller:	
Company:	
Phone:	
Email:	
Urgency: Low/Medium/High	Called ☐

Date: Time:	Message:
Caller:	
Company:	
Phone:	
Email:	
Urgency: Low/Medium/High	Called ☐
Date: Time:	Message:
Caller:	
Company:	
Phone:	
Email:	
Urgency: Low/Medium/High	Called ☐
Date: Time:	Message:
Caller:	
Company:	
Phone:	
Email:	
Urgency: Low/Medium/High	Called ☐
Date: Time:	Message:
Caller:	
Company:	
Phone:	
Email:	
Urgency: Low/Medium/High	Called ☐

Date: Time:	Message:
Caller:	
Company:	
Phone:	
Email:	
Urgency: Low/Medium/High	Called ☐
Date: Time:	Message:
Caller:	
Company:	
Phone:	
Email:	
Urgency: Low/Medium/High	Called ☐
Date: Time:	Message:
Caller:	
Company:	
Phone:	
Email:	
Urgency: Low/Medium/High	Called ☐
Date: Time:	Message:
Caller:	
Company:	
Phone:	
Email:	
Urgency: Low/Medium/High	Called ☐

Date: Time:	Message:
Caller:	
Company:	
Phone:	
Email:	
Urgency: Low/Medium/High	Called ☐
Date: Time:	Message:
Caller:	
Company:	
Phone:	
Email:	
Urgency: Low/Medium/High	Called ☐
Date: Time:	Message:
Caller:	
Company:	
Phone:	
Email:	
Urgency: Low/Medium/High	Called ☐
Date: Time:	Message:
Caller:	
Company:	
Phone:	
Email:	
Urgency: Low/Medium/High	Called ☐

Date: Time:	Message:
Caller:	
Company:	
Phone:	
Email:	
Urgency: Low/Medium/High	Called ☐
Date: Time:	Message:
Caller:	
Company:	
Phone:	
Email:	
Urgency: Low/Medium/High	Called ☐
Date: Time:	Message:
Caller:	
Company:	
Phone:	
Email:	
Urgency: Low/Medium/High	Called ☐
Date: Time:	Message:
Caller:	
Company:	
Phone:	
Email:	
Urgency: Low/Medium/High	Called ☐

Date: Time:	Message:
Caller:	
Company:	
Phone:	
Email:	
Urgency: Low/Medium/High	Called ☐
Date: Time:	Message:
Caller:	
Company:	
Phone:	
Email:	
Urgency: Low/Medium/High	Called ☐
Date: Time:	Message:
Caller:	
Company:	
Phone:	
Email:	
Urgency: Low/Medium/High	Called ☐
Date: Time:	Message:
Caller:	
Company:	
Phone:	
Email:	
Urgency: Low/Medium/High	Called ☐

Date: Time:	Message:
Caller:	
Company:	
Phone:	
Email:	
Urgency: Low/Medium/High	Called ☐
Date: Time:	Message:
Caller:	
Company:	
Phone:	
Email:	
Urgency: Low/Medium/High	Called ☐
Date: Time:	Message:
Caller:	
Company:	
Phone:	
Email:	
Urgency: Low/Medium/High	Called ☐
Date: Time:	Message:
Caller:	
Company:	
Phone:	
Email:	
Urgency: Low/Medium/High	Called ☐

Date: Time:	Message:
Caller:	
Company:	
Phone:	
Email:	
Urgency: Low/Medium/High	Called ☐
Date: Time:	Message:
Caller:	
Company:	
Phone:	
Email:	
Urgency: Low/Medium/High	Called ☐
Date: Time:	Message:
Caller:	
Company:	
Phone:	
Email:	
Urgency: Low/Medium/High	Called ☐
Date: Time:	Message:
Caller:	
Company:	
Phone:	
Email:	
Urgency: Low/Medium/High	Called ☐

Date: Time:	Message:
Caller:	
Company:	
Phone:	
Email:	
Urgency: Low/Medium/High	Called ☐
Date: Time:	Message:
Caller:	
Company:	
Phone:	
Email:	
Urgency: Low/Medium/High	Called ☐
Date: Time:	Message:
Caller:	
Company:	
Phone:	
Email:	
Urgency: Low/Medium/High	Called ☐
Date: Time:	Message:
Caller:	
Company:	
Phone:	
Email:	
Urgency: Low/Medium/High	Called ☐

Date: Time:	Message:
Caller:	
Company:	
Phone:	
Email:	
Urgency: Low/Medium/High	Called ☐
Date: Time:	Message:
Caller:	
Company:	
Phone:	
Email:	
Urgency: Low/Medium/High	Called ☐
Date: Time:	Message:
Caller:	
Company:	
Phone:	
Email:	
Urgency: Low/Medium/High	Called ☐
Date: Time:	Message:
Caller:	
Company:	
Phone:	
Email:	
Urgency: Low/Medium/High	Called ☐

Date: Time:	Message:
Caller:	
Company:	
Phone:	
Email:	
Urgency: Low/Medium/High	Called ☐
Date: Time:	Message:
Caller:	
Company:	
Phone:	
Email:	
Urgency: Low/Medium/High	Called ☐
Date: Time:	Message:
Caller:	
Company:	
Phone:	
Email:	
Urgency: Low/Medium/High	Called ☐
Date: Time:	Message:
Caller:	
Company:	
Phone:	
Email:	
Urgency: Low/Medium/High	Called ☐

Date: Time:	Message:
Caller:	
Company:	
Phone:	
Email:	
Urgency: Low/Medium/High	Called ☐
Date: Time:	Message:
Caller:	
Company:	
Phone:	
Email:	
Urgency: Low/Medium/High	Called ☐
Date: Time:	Message:
Caller:	
Company:	
Phone:	
Email:	
Urgency: Low/Medium/High	Called ☐
Date: Time:	Message:
Caller:	
Company:	
Phone:	
Email:	
Urgency: Low/Medium/High	Called ☐

Date: Time:	Message:
Caller:	
Company:	
Phone:	
Email:	
Urgency: Low/Medium/High	Called ☐
Date: Time:	Message:
Caller:	
Company:	
Phone:	
Email:	
Urgency: Low/Medium/High	Called ☐
Date: Time:	Message:
Caller:	
Company:	
Phone:	
Email:	
Urgency: Low/Medium/High	Called ☐
Date: Time:	Message:
Caller:	
Company:	
Phone:	
Email:	
Urgency: Low/Medium/High	Called ☐

Date: Time:	Message:
Caller:	
Company:	
Phone:	
Email:	
Urgency: Low/Medium/High	Called ☐

Date: Time:	Message:
Caller:	
Company:	
Phone:	
Email:	
Urgency: Low/Medium/High	Called ☐

Date: Time:	Message:
Caller:	
Company:	
Phone:	
Email:	
Urgency: Low/Medium/High	Called ☐

Date: Time:	Message:
Caller:	
Company:	
Phone:	
Email:	
Urgency: Low/Medium/High	Called ☐

Date: Time:	Message:
Caller:	
Company:	
Phone:	
Email:	
Urgency: Low/Medium/High	Called ☐
Date: Time:	Message:
Caller:	
Company:	
Phone:	
Email:	
Urgency: Low/Medium/High	Called ☐
Date: Time:	Message:
Caller:	
Company:	
Phone:	
Email:	
Urgency: Low/Medium/High	Called ☐
Date: Time:	Message:
Caller:	
Company:	
Phone:	
Email:	
Urgency: Low/Medium/High	Called ☐

Date: Time:	Message:
Caller:	
Company:	
Phone:	
Email:	
Urgency: Low/Medium/High	Called ☐
Date: Time:	Message:
Caller:	
Company:	
Phone:	
Email:	
Urgency: Low/Medium/High	Called ☐
Date: Time:	Message:
Caller:	
Company:	
Phone:	
Email:	
Urgency: Low/Medium/High	Called ☐
Date: Time:	Message:
Caller:	
Company:	
Phone:	
Email:	
Urgency: Low/Medium/High	Called ☐

Date: Time:	Message:
Caller:	
Company:	
Phone:	
Email:	
Urgency: Low/Medium/High	Called ☐
Date: Time:	Message:
Caller:	
Company:	
Phone:	
Email:	
Urgency: Low/Medium/High	Called ☐
Date: Time:	Message:
Caller:	
Company:	
Phone:	
Email:	
Urgency: Low/Medium/High	Called ☐
Date: Time:	Message:
Caller:	
Company:	
Phone:	
Email:	
Urgency: Low/Medium/High	Called ☐

Date: Time:	Message:
Caller:	
Company:	
Phone:	
Email:	
Urgency: Low/Medium/High	Called ☐
Date: Time:	Message:
Caller:	
Company:	
Phone:	
Email:	
Urgency: Low/Medium/High	Called ☐
Date: Time:	Message:
Caller:	
Company:	
Phone:	
Email:	
Urgency: Low/Medium/High	Called ☐
Date: Time:	Message:
Caller:	
Company:	
Phone:	
Email:	
Urgency: Low/Medium/High	Called ☐

Date: Time:	Message:
Caller:	
Company:	
Phone:	
Email:	
Urgency: Low/Medium/High	Called ☐
Date: Time:	Message:
Caller:	
Company:	
Phone:	
Email:	
Urgency: Low/Medium/High	Called ☐
Date: Time:	Message:
Caller:	
Company:	
Phone:	
Email:	
Urgency: Low/Medium/High	Called ☐
Date: Time:	Message:
Caller:	
Company:	
Phone:	
Email:	
Urgency: Low/Medium/High	Called ☐

Date: Time:	Message:
Caller:	
Company:	
Phone:	
Email:	
Urgency: Low/Medium/High	Called ☐
Date: Time:	Message:
Caller:	
Company:	
Phone:	
Email:	
Urgency: Low/Medium/High	Called ☐
Date: Time:	Message:
Caller:	
Company:	
Phone:	
Email:	
Urgency: Low/Medium/High	Called ☐
Date: Time:	Message:
Caller:	
Company:	
Phone:	
Email:	
Urgency: Low/Medium/High	Called ☐

Date: Time:	Message:
Caller:	
Company:	
Phone:	
Email:	
Urgency: Low/Medium/High	Called ☐
Date: Time:	Message:
Caller:	
Company:	
Phone:	
Email:	
Urgency: Low/Medium/High	Called ☐
Date: Time:	Message:
Caller:	
Company:	
Phone:	
Email:	
Urgency: Low/Medium/High	Called ☐
Date: Time:	Message:
Caller:	
Company:	
Phone:	
Email:	
Urgency: Low/Medium/High	Called ☐

Date: Time:	Message:
Caller:	
Company:	
Phone:	
Email:	
Urgency: Low/Medium/High	Called ☐
Date: Time:	Message:
Caller:	
Company:	
Phone:	
Email:	
Urgency: Low/Medium/High	Called ☐
Date: Time:	Message:
Caller:	
Company:	
Phone:	
Email:	
Urgency: Low/Medium/High	Called ☐
Date: Time:	Message:
Caller:	
Company:	
Phone:	
Email:	
Urgency: Low/Medium/High	Called ☐

Date: Time:	Message:
Caller:	
Company:	
Phone:	
Email:	
Urgency: Low/Medium/High	Called ☐
Date: Time:	Message:
Caller:	
Company:	
Phone:	
Email:	
Urgency: Low/Medium/High	Called ☐
Date: Time:	Message:
Caller:	
Company:	
Phone:	
Email:	
Urgency: Low/Medium/High	Called ☐
Date: Time:	Message:
Caller:	
Company:	
Phone:	
Email:	
Urgency: Low/Medium/High	Called ☐

Date: Time:	Message:
Caller:	
Company:	
Phone:	
Email:	
Urgency: Low/Medium/High	Called ☐
Date: Time:	Message:
Caller:	
Company:	
Phone:	
Email:	
Urgency: Low/Medium/High	Called ☐
Date: Time:	Message:
Caller:	
Company:	
Phone:	
Email:	
Urgency: Low/Medium/High	Called ☐
Date: Time:	Message:
Caller:	
Company:	
Phone:	
Email:	
Urgency: Low/Medium/High	Called ☐

Date: Time:	Message:
Caller:	
Company:	
Phone:	
Email:	
Urgency: Low/Medium/High	Called ☐
Date: Time:	Message:
Caller:	
Company:	
Phone:	
Email:	
Urgency: Low/Medium/High	Called ☐
Date: Time:	Message:
Caller:	
Company:	
Phone:	
Email:	
Urgency: Low/Medium/High	Called ☐
Date: Time:	Message:
Caller:	
Company:	
Phone:	
Email:	
Urgency: Low/Medium/High	Called ☐

Date: Time:	Message:
Caller:	
Company:	
Phone:	
Email:	
Urgency: Low/Medium/High	Called ☐
Date: Time:	Message:
Caller:	
Company:	
Phone:	
Email:	
Urgency: Low/Medium/High	Called ☐
Date: Time:	Message:
Caller:	
Company:	
Phone:	
Email:	
Urgency: Low/Medium/High	Called ☐
Date: Time:	Message:
Caller:	
Company:	
Phone:	
Email:	
Urgency: Low/Medium/High	Called ☐

Date: Time:	Message:
Caller:	
Company:	
Phone:	
Email:	
Urgency: Low/Medium/High	Called ☐
Date: Time:	Message:
Caller:	
Company:	
Phone:	
Email:	
Urgency: Low/Medium/High	Called ☐
Date: Time:	Message:
Caller:	
Company:	
Phone:	
Email:	
Urgency: Low/Medium/High	Called ☐
Date: Time:	Message:
Caller:	
Company:	
Phone:	
Email:	
Urgency: Low/Medium/High	Called ☐

Date: Time:	Message:
Caller:	
Company:	
Phone:	
Email:	
Urgency: Low/Medium/High	Called ☐
Date: Time:	Message:
Caller:	
Company:	
Phone:	
Email:	
Urgency: Low/Medium/High	Called ☐
Date: Time:	Message:
Caller:	
Company:	
Phone:	
Email:	
Urgency: Low/Medium/High	Called ☐
Date: Time:	Message:
Caller:	
Company:	
Phone:	
Email:	
Urgency: Low/Medium/High	Called ☐

Date: Time:	Message:
Caller:	
Company:	
Phone:	
Email:	
Urgency: Low/Medium/High	Called ☐
Date: Time:	Message:
Caller:	
Company:	
Phone:	
Email:	
Urgency: Low/Medium/High	Called ☐
Date: Time:	Message:
Caller:	
Company:	
Phone:	
Email:	
Urgency: Low/Medium/High	Called ☐
Date: Time:	Message:
Caller:	
Company:	
Phone:	
Email:	
Urgency: Low/Medium/High	Called ☐

Date: Time:	Message:
Caller:	
Company:	
Phone:	
Email:	
Urgency: Low/Medium/High	Called ☐
Date: Time:	Message:
Caller:	
Company:	
Phone:	
Email:	
Urgency: Low/Medium/High	Called ☐
Date: Time:	Message:
Caller:	
Company:	
Phone:	
Email:	
Urgency: Low/Medium/High	Called ☐
Date: Time:	Message:
Caller:	
Company:	
Phone:	
Email:	
Urgency: Low/Medium/High	Called ☐

Date: Time:	Message:
Caller:	
Company:	
Phone:	
Email:	
Urgency: Low/Medium/High	Called ☐
Date: Time:	Message:
Caller:	
Company:	
Phone:	
Email:	
Urgency: Low/Medium/High	Called ☐
Date: Time:	Message:
Caller:	
Company:	
Phone:	
Email:	
Urgency: Low/Medium/High	Called ☐
Date: Time:	Message:
Caller:	
Company:	
Phone:	
Email:	
Urgency: Low/Medium/High	Called ☐

Date: Time:	Message:
Caller:	
Company:	
Phone:	
Email:	
Urgency: Low/Medium/High	Called ☐
Date: Time:	Message:
Caller:	
Company:	
Phone:	
Email:	
Urgency: Low/Medium/High	Called ☐
Date: Time:	Message:
Caller:	
Company:	
Phone:	
Email:	
Urgency: Low/Medium/High	Called ☐
Date: Time:	Message:
Caller:	
Company:	
Phone:	
Email:	
Urgency: Low/Medium/High	Called ☐

Date: Time:	Message:
Caller:	
Company:	
Phone:	
Email:	
Urgency: Low/Medium/High	Called ☐
Date: Time:	Message:
Caller:	
Company:	
Phone:	
Email:	
Urgency: Low/Medium/High	Called ☐
Date: Time:	Message:
Caller:	
Company:	
Phone:	
Email:	
Urgency: Low/Medium/High	Called ☐
Date: Time:	Message:
Caller:	
Company:	
Phone:	
Email:	
Urgency: Low/Medium/High	Called ☐

Date: Time:	Message:
Caller:	
Company:	
Phone:	
Email:	
Urgency: Low/Medium/High	Called ☐
Date: Time:	Message:
Caller:	
Company:	
Phone:	
Email:	
Urgency: Low/Medium/High	Called ☐
Date: Time:	Message:
Caller:	
Company:	
Phone:	
Email:	
Urgency: Low/Medium/High	Called ☐
Date: Time:	Message:
Caller:	
Company:	
Phone:	
Email:	
Urgency: Low/Medium/High	Called ☐

Date: Time:	Message:
Caller:	
Company:	
Phone:	
Email:	
Urgency: Low/Medium/High	Called ☐
Date: Time:	Message:
Caller:	
Company:	
Phone:	
Email:	
Urgency: Low/Medium/High	Called ☐
Date: Time:	Message:
Caller:	
Company:	
Phone:	
Email:	
Urgency: Low/Medium/High	Called ☐
Date: Time:	Message:
Caller:	
Company:	
Phone:	
Email:	
Urgency: Low/Medium/High	Called ☐

Date: Time:	Message:
Caller:	
Company:	
Phone:	
Email:	
Urgency: Low/Medium/High	Called ☐
Date: Time:	Message:
Caller:	
Company:	
Phone:	
Email:	
Urgency: Low/Medium/High	Called ☐
Date: Time:	Message:
Caller:	
Company:	
Phone:	
Email:	
Urgency: Low/Medium/High	Called ☐
Date: Time:	Message:
Caller:	
Company:	
Phone:	
Email:	
Urgency: Low/Medium/High	Called ☐

Date: Time:	Message:
Caller:	
Company:	
Phone:	
Email:	
Urgency: Low/Medium/High	Called ☐
Date: Time:	Message:
Caller:	
Company:	
Phone:	
Email:	
Urgency: Low/Medium/High	Called ☐
Date: Time:	Message:
Caller:	
Company:	
Phone:	
Email:	
Urgency: Low/Medium/High	Called ☐
Date: Time:	Message:
Caller:	
Company:	
Phone:	
Email:	
Urgency: Low/Medium/High	Called ☐

Date: Time:	Message:
Caller:	
Company:	
Phone:	
Email:	
Urgency: Low/Medium/High	Called ☐
Date: Time:	Message:
Caller:	
Company:	
Phone:	
Email:	
Urgency: Low/Medium/High	Called ☐
Date: Time:	Message:
Caller:	
Company:	
Phone:	
Email:	
Urgency: Low/Medium/High	Called ☐
Date: Time:	Message:
Caller:	
Company:	
Phone:	
Email:	
Urgency: Low/Medium/High	Called ☐

Date: Time:	Message:
Caller:	
Company:	
Phone:	
Email:	
Urgency: Low/Medium/High	Called ☐
Date: Time:	Message:
Caller:	
Company:	
Phone:	
Email:	
Urgency: Low/Medium/High	Called ☐
Date: Time:	Message:
Caller:	
Company:	
Phone:	
Email:	
Urgency: Low/Medium/High	Called ☐
Date: Time:	Message:
Caller:	
Company:	
Phone:	
Email:	
Urgency: Low/Medium/High	Called ☐

Date: Time:	Message:
Caller:	
Company:	
Phone:	
Email:	
Urgency: Low/Medium/High	Called ☐
Date: Time:	Message:
Caller:	
Company:	
Phone:	
Email:	
Urgency: Low/Medium/High	Called ☐
Date: Time:	Message:
Caller:	
Company:	
Phone:	
Email:	
Urgency: Low/Medium/High	Called ☐
Date: Time:	Message:
Caller:	
Company:	
Phone:	
Email:	
Urgency: Low/Medium/High	Called ☐

Date: Time:	Message:
Caller:	
Company:	
Phone:	
Email:	
Urgency: Low/Medium/High	Called ☐
Date: Time:	Message:
Caller:	
Company:	
Phone:	
Email:	
Urgency: Low/Medium/High	Called ☐
Date: Time:	Message:
Caller:	
Company:	
Phone:	
Email:	
Urgency: Low/Medium/High	Called ☐
Date: Time:	Message:
Caller:	
Company:	
Phone:	
Email:	
Urgency: Low/Medium/High	Called ☐

Date: Time:	Message:
Caller:	
Company:	
Phone:	
Email:	
Urgency: Low/Medium/High	Called ☐
Date: Time:	Message:
Caller:	
Company:	
Phone:	
Email:	
Urgency: Low/Medium/High	Called ☐
Date: Time:	Message:
Caller:	
Company:	
Phone:	
Email:	
Urgency: Low/Medium/High	Called ☐
Date: Time:	Message:
Caller:	
Company:	
Phone:	
Email:	
Urgency: Low/Medium/High	Called ☐

Date: Time:	Message:
Caller:	
Company:	
Phone:	
Email:	
Urgency: Low/Medium/High	Called ☐
Date: Time:	Message:
Caller:	
Company:	
Phone:	
Email:	
Urgency: Low/Medium/High	Called ☐
Date: Time:	Message:
Caller:	
Company:	
Phone:	
Email:	
Urgency: Low/Medium/High	Called ☐
Date: Time:	Message:
Caller:	
Company:	
Phone:	
Email:	
Urgency: Low/Medium/High	Called ☐

Date: Time:	Message:
Caller:	
Company:	
Phone:	
Email:	
Urgency: Low/Medium/High	Called ☐
Date: Time:	Message:
Caller:	
Company:	
Phone:	
Email:	
Urgency: Low/Medium/High	Called ☐
Date: Time:	Message:
Caller:	
Company:	
Phone:	
Email:	
Urgency: Low/Medium/High	Called ☐
Date: Time:	Message:
Caller:	
Company:	
Phone:	
Email:	
Urgency: Low/Medium/High	Called ☐

Date: Time:	Message:
Caller:	
Company:	
Phone:	
Email:	
Urgency: Low/Medium/High	Called ☐
Date: Time:	Message:
Caller:	
Company:	
Phone:	
Email:	
Urgency: Low/Medium/High	Called ☐
Date: Time:	Message:
Caller:	
Company:	
Phone:	
Email:	
Urgency: Low/Medium/High	Called ☐
Date: Time:	Message:
Caller:	
Company:	
Phone:	
Email:	
Urgency: Low/Medium/High	Called ☐

Date: Time:	Message:
Caller:	
Company:	
Phone:	
Email:	
Urgency: Low/Medium/High	Called ☐
Date: Time:	Message:
Caller:	
Company:	
Phone:	
Email:	
Urgency: Low/Medium/High	Called ☐
Date: Time:	Message:
Caller:	
Company:	
Phone:	
Email:	
Urgency: Low/Medium/High	Called ☐
Date: Time:	Message:
Caller:	
Company:	
Phone:	
Email:	
Urgency: Low/Medium/High	Called ☐

Date: Time:	Message:
Caller:	
Company:	
Phone:	
Email:	
Urgency: Low/Medium/High	Called ☐
Date: Time:	Message:
Caller:	
Company:	
Phone:	
Email:	
Urgency: Low/Medium/High	Called ☐
Date: Time:	Message:
Caller:	
Company:	
Phone:	
Email:	
Urgency: Low/Medium/High	Called ☐
Date: Time:	Message:
Caller:	
Company:	
Phone:	
Email:	
Urgency: Low/Medium/High	Called ☐

Date: Time:	Message:
Caller:	
Company:	
Phone:	
Email:	
Urgency: Low/Medium/High	Called ☐
Date: Time:	Message:
Caller:	
Company:	
Phone:	
Email:	
Urgency: Low/Medium/High	Called ☐
Date: Time:	Message:
Caller:	
Company:	
Phone:	
Email:	
Urgency: Low/Medium/High	Called ☐
Date: Time:	Message:
Caller:	
Company:	
Phone:	
Email:	
Urgency: Low/Medium/High	Called ☐

Date: Time:	Message:
Caller:	
Company:	
Phone:	
Email:	
Urgency: Low/Medium/High	Called ☐
Date: Time:	Message:
Caller:	
Company:	
Phone:	
Email:	
Urgency: Low/Medium/High	Called ☐
Date: Time:	Message:
Caller:	
Company:	
Phone:	
Email:	
Urgency: Low/Medium/High	Called ☐
Date: Time:	Message:
Caller:	
Company:	
Phone:	
Email:	
Urgency: Low/Medium/High	Called ☐

Date:　　　　Time:	Message:
Caller:	
Company:	
Phone:	
Email:	
Urgency: Low/Medium/High	Called ☐
Date:　　　　Time:	Message:
Caller:	
Company:	
Phone:	
Email:	
Urgency: Low/Medium/High	Called ☐
Date:　　　　Time:	Message:
Caller:	
Company:	
Phone:	
Email:	
Urgency: Low/Medium/High	Called ☐
Date:　　　　Time:	Message:
Caller:	
Company:	
Phone:	
Email:	
Urgency: Low/Medium/High	Called ☐

Date: Time:	Message:
Caller:	
Company:	
Phone:	
Email:	
Urgency: Low/Medium/High	Called ☐
Date: Time:	Message:
Caller:	
Company:	
Phone:	
Email:	
Urgency: Low/Medium/High	Called ☐
Date: Time:	Message:
Caller:	
Company:	
Phone:	
Email:	
Urgency: Low/Medium/High	Called ☐
Date: Time:	Message:
Caller:	
Company:	
Phone:	
Email:	
Urgency: Low/Medium/High	Called ☐

Date: Time:	Message:
Caller:	
Company:	
Phone:	
Email:	
Urgency: Low/Medium/High	Called ☐
Date: Time:	Message:
Caller:	
Company:	
Phone:	
Email:	
Urgency: Low/Medium/High	Called ☐
Date: Time:	Message:
Caller:	
Company:	
Phone:	
Email:	
Urgency: Low/Medium/High	Called ☐
Date: Time:	Message:
Caller:	
Company:	
Phone:	
Email:	
Urgency: Low/Medium/High	Called ☐

Date: Time:	Message:
Caller:	
Company:	
Phone:	
Email:	
Urgency: Low/Medium/High	Called ☐
Date: Time:	Message:
Caller:	
Company:	
Phone:	
Email:	
Urgency: Low/Medium/High	Called ☐
Date: Time:	Message:
Caller:	
Company:	
Phone:	
Email:	
Urgency: Low/Medium/High	Called ☐
Date: Time:	Message:
Caller:	
Company:	
Phone:	
Email:	
Urgency: Low/Medium/High	Called ☐

Date: Time:	Message:
Caller:	
Company:	
Phone:	
Email:	
Urgency: Low/Medium/High	Called ☐
Date: Time:	Message:
Caller:	
Company:	
Phone:	
Email:	
Urgency: Low/Medium/High	Called ☐
Date: Time:	Message:
Caller:	
Company:	
Phone:	
Email:	
Urgency: Low/Medium/High	Called ☐
Date: Time:	Message:
Caller:	
Company:	
Phone:	
Email:	
Urgency: Low/Medium/High	Called ☐

Date: Time:	Message:
Caller:	
Company:	
Phone:	
Email:	
Urgency: Low/Medium/High	Called ☐

Date: Time:	Message:
Caller:	
Company:	
Phone:	
Email:	
Urgency: Low/Medium/High	Called ☐

Date: Time:	Message:
Caller:	
Company:	
Phone:	
Email:	
Urgency: Low/Medium/High	Called ☐

Date: Time:	Message:
Caller:	
Company:	
Phone:	
Email:	
Urgency: Low/Medium/High	Called ☐

Date: Time:	Message:
Caller:	
Company:	
Phone:	
Email:	
Urgency: Low/Medium/High	Called ☐
Date: Time:	Message:
Caller:	
Company:	
Phone:	
Email:	
Urgency: Low/Medium/High	Called ☐
Date: Time:	Message:
Caller:	
Company:	
Phone:	
Email:	
Urgency: Low/Medium/High	Called ☐
Date: Time:	Message:
Caller:	
Company:	
Phone:	
Email:	
Urgency: Low/Medium/High	Called ☐

Date: Time:	Message:
Caller:	
Company:	
Phone:	
Email:	
Urgency: Low/Medium/High	Called ☐
Date: Time:	Message:
Caller:	
Company:	
Phone:	
Email:	
Urgency: Low/Medium/High	Called ☐
Date: Time:	Message:
Caller:	
Company:	
Phone:	
Email:	
Urgency: Low/Medium/High	Called ☐
Date: Time:	Message:
Caller:	
Company:	
Phone:	
Email:	
Urgency: Low/Medium/High	Called ☐

Date: Time:	Message:
Caller:	
Company:	
Phone:	
Email:	
Urgency: Low/Medium/High	Called ☐
Date: Time:	Message:
Caller:	
Company:	
Phone:	
Email:	
Urgency: Low/Medium/High	Called ☐
Date: Time:	Message:
Caller:	
Company:	
Phone:	
Email:	
Urgency: Low/Medium/High	Called ☐
Date: Time:	Message:
Caller:	
Company:	
Phone:	
Email:	
Urgency: Low/Medium/High	Called ☐

CPSIA information can be obtained
at www.ICGtesting.com
Printed in the USA
LVHW050723231119
638071LV00008B/3710/P